# Surviving Grief

## The Path to Your Resurrection

LEONARDO TAVARES

# Surviving Grief
## The Path to Your Resurrection

# SURVIVING GRIEF

May this book provide a hug,
A comfort to the wounded hearts,
May it bring the certainty
That pain can be overcome with love.

There is no definitive goodbye
For the connection we have with those we love
Goes beyond death, transcends time and space,
And it becomes an eternal source of inspiration and love.

May the longing be transformed into joy,
And may memories be a treasure,
May tears be wiped away by love,
And may light shine on the path of those who suffer.

This book is a tribute to
All those who have passed away
And to all those who are facing grief,
May it be a source of comfort and hope.

And even in the most difficult moments,
May we find the strength and courage
To move forward, to honor the memory of those we love,
And to live our lives with joy, gratitude, and love.

*In memory of my sweet wife Fernanda Tavares.*

# CONTENTS

# FOREWORD

I wrote this book to share with you, my readers, what I have experienced and learned through much suffering and the passage of time.

The loss of someone important can be one of the most difficult experiences in life. Grief is a natural and healthy response to such a loss, but it can be a very painful and challenging process. In "Surviving Grief", we will explore together the different aspects of the grieving process and how to deal with it in healthy and constructive ways.

You will also find valuable information about the stages of grief, how to cope with loss, the impact of grief on mental health, the importance of social support in the grieving process, and much more.

I hope this book can bring comfort, hope, and peace to those who are going through the grieving process. May it remind them that they are not alone, and that it is possible to find light even in the darkest situations.

Always remember that love is stronger than death, and love never dies.

With hope and gratitude,

Leonardo Tavares

# CHAPTER 1

# THE BEGINNING OF PAIN

EVEN IN
THE DARKEST
OF NIGHTS,
THERE IS A
RADIANT LIGHT
WITHIN YOU,
GUIDING YOUR
STEPS TOWARD
HEALING.

Life is made of ups and downs. Moments of joy and happiness are balanced by moments of sadness and pain. Unfortunately, loss is an inevitable part of life. At some point, we will all experience the pain of losing someone we love.

The beginning of pain is a very difficult and confusing phase. When we receive the news of the loss, we often feel dazed and directionless. The pain is intense and seems unbearable. It's like the ground has disappeared from under our feet.

At first, it can be hard to believe that the person we love is gone. We may feel like we're in a nightmare and can't wake up. It's a feeling of unreality that seems never to pass.

Denial is one of the first reactions we experience in the face of loss. It's a form of emotional protection, an attempt to shield ourselves from pain and suffering. It's as if we can't accept the reality of the loss.

But over time, reality begins to set in. The pain starts to become stronger and more intense. Sadness and longing hit us hard, and the reality starts to sink in. It's at this point that the pain becomes sharper, more intense, and harder to bear.

The pain of grief is a pain unlike any other. It's a deep pain that affects us on all levels: physical, emotional, mental, and spiritual. It's as if our world has collapsed, and nothing else makes sense.

It's common to feel a range of intense and contradictory emotions during the grieving process. We can feel sad, angry, confused, desperate, lost, among other things. Sometimes we can even feel relief, especially if the person who passed away was suffering or in a difficult situation.

These emotions can be overwhelming and difficult to handle. Sometimes, we can feel like we are on the verge of madness. But it is important to remember that these emotions are normal and are part of the grieving process.

Each person deals with grief in a unique way. There is no right or wrong way to feel or express the pain. Each of us has the right to experience grief in our own way.

It is important to remember that the grieving process is not linear. There is no clear progression of stages that we must follow. Instead, the grieving process is a complex and multifaceted process that involves ups and downs.

Sometimes, we may feel better for a while, only to be hit again by sadness and longing. It is a process of highs and lows, of progress and setbacks.

The beginning of pain is just the start of the grieving process. It is a moment of shock, denial, and confusion. It is the moment when reality begins to impose itself, and the pain begins to become more real and intense.

It is important to allow yourself to feel the pain and not try to suppress or deny it. It is necessary to find healthy ways to cope with the pain and suffering. This may include crying, talking to friends and family, seeking professional help, expressing the pain through art or writing, among other things.

There is no right or wrong way to deal with grief. Each person has their own way of coping with pain. It is important to respect and honor your own grieving process and allow yourself time to heal.

In this time of pain, it is common to question the meaning of life and the existence of a greater plan. These questions can be difficult to answer, but it is important to seek meaning and purpose in life, even in the face of loss.

Loss is an inevitable part of life, but the love and memories we shared with the departed person remain with us forever. It is important to honor the memory of the loved one and keep their presence alive in our hearts.

Remember that we are not alone. There are many people around us who love and care for us. Seek support and comfort whenever needed.

# CHAPTER 2

# THE STAGES OF GRIEF

GRIEF IS AN INTRICATE VOYAGE, AND EACH STAGE IS A FOOTPRINT TOWARD INNER TRANQUILITY.

When a person experiences a significant loss, such as the death of a loved one, it's common to go through a series of emotional stages, which are known as the stages of grief. Although not everyone experiences all of these stages, or in the same order, understanding these phases can help the person to understand their own feelings and what to expect on their grief journey.

## Denial

The first stage of grief is denial. In this stage, the person may refuse to believe that the loss has really happened. This can be accompanied by feelings of shock, confusion, and disorientation. It's common for people to feel stunned and unable to fully process what has happened.

## Anger

Anger is another common stage of grief. In this stage, the person may feel irritated and frustrated. They may look for someone to blame for their loss or be angry at the person who died. They may feel like they've been wronged or that life is unfair.

## Bargaining

In the bargaining stage, the person may try to make deals with God or with life to avoid the pain of the loss. They may wonder what they could have done differently to prevent their loved one's death. It's common for people to feel desperate to regain what has been lost and therefore try to negotiate with their emotions.

## Depression

Depression is another stage of grief. In this stage, the person may feel profound sadness and hopelessness. They may feel alone and isolated, even when surrounded by friends and family. Depression can be accompanied by crying, insomnia, loss of appetite, and fatigue.

## Acceptance

Finally, the last stage of the grief stages is acceptance. In this stage, the person begins to accept the reality of the loss and find a way to move forward. They may start to plan for the future without the person who died and find meaning in their life again.

Although not everyone goes through all of these stages, and some people may go through them in a different order, it is important to remember that grief is a personal and unique process for each individual. There is no right or wrong way to feel or go through this process. It is important to allow yourself to feel all the emotions that arise and find ways to cope with them in a healthy way.

In the next chapters, I will present each stage of the grieving process and provide the necessary recommendations to help you navigate through what is one of the most difficult periods of our lives.

# CHAPTER 3
# DENIAL

CONFRONTING
THE TRUTH
IS THE INITIAL
STRIDE TO
TRANSMUTE
DENIAL INTO
FORTITUDE.

When we lose someone we love, it is natural to have difficulties dealing with the reality of the loss. In many cases, denial is one of the first reactions that arise. Denial is a form of self-protection, an attempt to maintain the illusion that the person is still present in our life. However, denial can become an obstacle to the grieving process and to our ability to cope with loss.

Denial is a common stage of the grieving process. When we lose someone, it is difficult to accept the reality of the loss. It is normal to feel that the person is still present in our life, or to hope that they will come back. In this stage, it may be hard to believe that the loss is permanent.

Denial can manifest in various ways. Some people may refuse to accept the reality of the loss, ignoring the facts or avoiding thinking about it. Others may act as if nothing has happened, maintaining normal routines and avoiding talking about the loss. Denial can even manifest as a form of anger or rebellion, when we do not want to accept the loss and look for someone or something to blame.

Denial can be a temporary defense mechanism, but it can become an obstacle to the grieving process. When we deny the reality of loss, we are hindering our ability to process the emotions and feelings related to the loss. We are postponing the pain and suffering, which can prolong the grieving process and make recovery more difficult.

It is important to understand that denial is a normal stage of the grieving process, but it needs to be faced and overcome in order to move forward. Acceptance of the loss is an important stage of the grieving process, which allows us to begin rebuilding our lives without the departed person. When we accept the loss, we are opening up space to feel the emotions and process the feelings of sadness and longing. We are allowing the grieving process to follow its natural course.

There are various strategies that can help to deal with denial in the grieving process. Finding healthy ways to cope with emotions is crucial. Engaging in physical activities such as walking or yoga can help to reduce stress and anxiety. Expressing oneself artistically through writing, music or visual arts can be a powerful way to process emotions and find meaning in the loss.

Seeking help and support from close ones, friends, and family can aid in adapting to the loss. It is important to talk about the loss and express emotions and feelings related to it. Therapy can also be a useful tool to deal with denial and other stages of grief.

Lastly, participating in support groups for people going through the same process can be a valuable source of support. Finding other individuals who are going through the same process can help to feel understood and supported, as well as offer the opportunity to share life experiences.

# CHAPTER 4
# **ANGER**

ANGER IS AKIN
TO AN INTERNAL
FLAME, TRANSMUTE
IT INTO
THE FUEL
FOR YOUR
GROWTH.

Anger is one of the strongest emotions we experience when going through the grieving process. It can arise for different reasons, from feeling a sense of injustice over the loss to frustration over not having had the opportunity to say goodbye. Whatever the cause, anger can be intense and difficult to deal with.

When we lose someone, we often feel like we have no control over anything. Life seems to have played a trick on us and left us in an unexpected and unfair situation. Anger can be a natural response to this sense of powerlessness and helplessness.

Moreover, anger is often directed at other people. We may feel anger towards the doctors who couldn't save our loved one, towards the family members who weren't there, or even towards the person who died for leaving us alone. It's important to remember that these feelings are not good or bad, they simply exist and need to be processed.

However, anger can become an obstacle to the grieving process if it's not expressed and understood in a healthy way. If we hold anger inside us, it can turn into resentment and bitterness and end up affecting our relationships with others and our own mental health.

One way to deal with anger is to allow ourselves to feel it. It's normal and healthy to feel anger in the face of a significant loss. We should allow ourselves to experience this emotion, express it in a safe way, and understand it. We can seek professional help, talk to friends and family, or even write about what we're feeling. The key is not to let anger control our actions and our lives.

Another way to deal with anger is to find ways to channel it in a positive way. We can use this energy to change aspects of our lives that bother us, to do physical activities or volunteer work, or even to create something new. Anger can be a source of motivation if we know how to use it in a healthy way.

Know that anger is not and will not be permanent. It can arise intensely in some moments and decrease in others. It's normal for the emotion to come in waves throughout the grieving process. The important thing is to allow ourselves to feel it and deal with it in a healthy way, so that we can move forward in the healing process.

# CHAPTER 5
# BARGAINING

IN THE PURSUIT
OF ANSWERS,
WE UNEARTH
STRENGTH
TO EMBRACE
WHAT WE
CANNOT ALTER.

Grief is a complex and often painful process that can lead to a range of difficult emotions. One of these emotions is bargaining, which refers to an attempt to negotiate with the pain of loss in search of solutions or ways to avoid it.

Bargaining can arise at different times in the grieving process and can be an attempt to avoid the pain and sadness that come with loss. It is a way of seeking a sense of control at a time when many things seem to be out of control.

Bargaining can manifest in various ways. Some people may try to negotiate with God or life for their loved one to come back or for the pain to be relieved. Others may make promises or sacrifices, such as committing to changing their habits or being more attentive to others, in exchange for relief from the pain.

Although bargaining may be a temporary way of coping with the pain, it is important to understand that, in the end, it does not offer a real solution to the loss. Death is an inevitable part of life, and no amount of negotiation or bargaining can change that.

It is important to remember that the grieving process is different for each person and that there is no "right" way to deal with it. Some people may experience bargaining as a natural part of the grieving process, while others may not feel this emotion or experience it differently.

However, it is important that people in grief are not judged or criticized for their emotions or reactions. Each individual needs to be respected in their own grieving process and have space to experience their emotions without fear or shame.

Therapy can be a useful way to deal with bargaining and other difficult emotions that may arise during the grieving process. An experienced therapist can help the grieving person explore their emotions safely and find healthy ways to cope with loss. This does not mean that we should stop missing or forget those who have passed away. On the contrary, we need to learn to live with the pain and find new meaning in life without the presence of that person. This may take time, but it is an important step on the path to healing.

In addition to therapy, there are other ways to deal with bargaining and other difficult emotions of grief. Some find it helpful to focus on the good things the loved one brought to their lives and remember the good times they shared. Others may find comfort in activities that help them connect with their emotions, such as writing a journal or practicing meditation.

Ultimately, bargaining may be a natural part of the grieving process, but it is important to remember that it does not offer a real solution to loss. It is important for people in grief to have space and support to process their emotions and find healthy ways to cope with their pain.

There is no timetable or roadmap for grief, but believe that, over time, it is possible to find meaning in loss and move forward.

# CHAPTER 6

# DEPRESSION

IN THE BLEAKEST
MOMENTS,
REMEMBER
THAT YOU POSSESS
THE FORTITUDE
TO BRAVE
THE TEMPEST.

Losing someone we deeply love can be one of the most challenging experiences we may face in life; it is devastating. It is natural to feel sadness, distress, and even depression in the grieving process, and each person deals with this process in a different way. Some people may go through this period with ease, while others may feel like they are sinking into a bottomless pit.

Depression is one of the most common symptoms of grief. It can manifest in various different ways, from a constant feeling of sadness and despair to losing interest in activities that were once enjoyable. Some people may also feel a sense of emptiness or lack of purpose in their lives.

It is important to understand that depression in grief is a natural reaction to loss and should not be ignored or minimized. If you are experiencing grief-related depression, seeking professional help is essential. A psychologist or therapist can help you deal with your feelings and develop coping skills for grieving.

Grief-related depression can be treated in various different ways, depending on the severity of symptoms and individual needs. Cognitive-behavioral therapy is a common treatment that focuses on changing negative thought patterns and behaviors associated with depression. Interpersonal therapy is another approach that focuses on interpersonal relationships and how they affect mental health.

In addition to therapy, there are other things you can do to cope with grief-related depression. It is important to take care of yourself both physically and emotionally. This includes eating a healthy diet, exercising regularly, finding new hobbies, getting enough sleep, and avoiding substances that may worsen depression symptoms.

It is also crucial to seek the support of friends and family who can help you during this difficult time. They can offer advice, active listening, or simply be there when you need someone to talk to.

The most important thing to remember is that grieving is a unique process for each person, and there is no defined timeframe for overcoming it. It is normal to feel a range of different emotions during this period, and there may be ups and downs on the road to recovery. But with professional help, self-care, and the support of loved ones, it is possible to overcome grief-related depression and find a new sense of purpose in life.

# CHAPTER 7

# ACCEPTANCE

IN ACCEPTANCE,
WE UNEARTH
THE FREEDOM
TO PERSEVERE
AND THE VIGOR
TO EMBARK
ANEW.

When we lose someone we love, it's common to go through a period of denial, anger, sadness, and depression as we saw in the previous chapters. We may question why this happened to us, feel that we don't deserve this pain, or think that life is unfair. But at some point, we need to face reality and come to terms with the loss.

Acceptance is one of the most difficult and challenging steps in the grieving process. It's a stage that can take a long period of time, as we often need to deal with a flood of emotions before we can get used to the reality of the loss. But when we reach this point, it's possible to feel a sense of relief and a weight being lifted off our shoulders.

Accepting the loss doesn't mean that we're forgetting the person we loved or that we're putting aside our grief. On the contrary, it's a process of understanding that the person is gone and that we need to find a way to move forward. It's important to understand that the grieving process is an individual journey, and each person may take their time to accept the loss.

There are many ways to cope with acceptance of the loss. Some people prefer to talk about the person who's gone, reminisce about happy moments and keep their memory alive. Others prefer to dedicate themselves to new activities, new hobbies, new relationships, or new projects to help them find a new purpose in life.

Accepting the loss also means forgiving ourselves and others. Often, we may feel guilty about things that happened before the loss, or we may feel angry about situations that we can't control. But it's important to remember that these emotions don't help us move forward, and at some point, we need to forgive ourselves and others to find inner peace.

Acceptance can be a difficult and painful process, but it's an important step in finding inner peace and healing. It's a process of allowing emotions to be felt and processed, so we can move forward and find a new purpose in life.

It's important to remember that the process of acceptance may take time, and each person may cope with the loss differently. Be kind to yourself, seek support, practice activities that bring you pleasure, and allow the grieving journey to be a less painful experience. With time, love, and support, it's possible to find acceptance and healing.

# CHAPTER 8

# THE IMPORTANCE OF ALLOWING YOURSELF TO FEEL

ALLOW YOURSELF
TO FEEL,
FOR IN THE
PROCESSING
OF EMOTIONS,
THE JOURNEY
OF HEALING
BEGINS.

Grief is a process that involves a variety of intense and conflicting emotions. It is common for the grieving person to experience feelings of sadness, anger, guilt, anxiety, loneliness, and even relief. These emotions can be very intense, and often people try to repress or ignore them, believing that it will make them feel better. However, denying emotions can lead to long-term emotional and physical problems. It is therefore important to allow yourself to feel all the emotions that arise during the grieving process.

Some people believe that they need to be strong and stay firm during grief, but this can be detrimental. Allowing yourself to feel all emotions is an important part of the healing process. It is normal to feel sadness, anger, guilt, and other negative feelings after the loss of a loved one. Ignoring these feelings or trying to suppress them can only make the situation worse.

Accepting and dealing with emotions can be difficult, but it is necessary. One way to do this is to try to express these feelings. Some people prefer to talk to friends or family, while others prefer to write in a journal or seek the help of a mental health professional. The important thing is to find a healthy way to express emotions and share feelings with someone who can listen without judgment.

In addition to expressing emotions, it is also important to acknowledge and validate feelings. It is common for people to judge themselves for feeling anger or sadness, but these feelings are normal and should not be ignored. Validating these feelings can help the grieving person feel less isolated and alone in their suffering.

However, it is important to remember that while it is important to allow yourself to feel all emotions, it is also important to take care of your physical and mental health. This may include activities such as physical exercise, hobbies, meditation, adequate sleep, and healthy eating. Taking care of yourself can help reduce the stress and anxiety that often accompany the grieving process.

Finding healthy ways to deal with emotions can be a challenge, but it is an important step in the healing process. It is important to allow yourself to feel all the emotions that arise, without judgment, and find healthy ways to express and deal with them. Doing so can help the grieving person find some comfort and meaning in their loss.

# CHAPTER 9

# THE SUPPORT OF FAMILY AND FRIENDS

WITHIN
THE TENDER HANDS
OF FAMILY
AND FRIENDS,
SOLACE
AND WARMTH
ARE FOUND AMID
TRYING TIMES.

The support of family and friends is crucial for over-coming grief and emotional pain that come with the loss of a loved one. When we experience loss, it's common to feel a sense of loneliness and isolation, but it's important to remember that we are not alone.

Close family members and friends are essential at this time. They can offer comfort, emotional and practical support, and a loving presence that helps us to face the challenges of grief. Through small acts of kindness and a supportive shoulder to cry on, our loved ones can help us find the strength to move forward.

However, it's important to remember that it's not always easy to ask for help, and each person deals with grief in their own unique way. Some people prefer to withdraw and deal with their pain alone, while others need more constant and present support. Regardless of what you need, it's important to communicate with your loved ones and let them know how they can help.

Remember that not everyone close to us knows how to help or deal with our pain. Therefore, it's important to have empathy and understand that everyone has their own way of dealing with loss and emotional pain. If someone doesn't know what to say or how to act, it's important to remember that it doesn't mean they don't care, but rather that they are dealing with the situation in the best way they can.

Seek support from other sources as well, such as support groups or therapy. These tools can be essential for dealing with emotional pain and finding the strength to move forward.

The grieving process is not something that needs to be faced alone. There are many people and resources available to help overcome the pain and find a new path.

# CHAPTER 10

# THE IMPORTANCE OF TAKING CARE OF YOURSELF

SELF-CARE
IS THE MOST
AFFECTIONATE
GESTURE WE CAN
BESTOW UPON
THE WOUNDED
HEART.

When going through the grieving process, we often forget to take care of ourselves. We become so focused on the pain and suffering that we feel that we end up neglecting our own health and well-being. However, taking care of yourself during grief is crucial to help you overcome this difficult phase.

Taking care of yourself doesn't just mean taking care of your physical health, but also your mental and emotional health. It's important to remember that grief can affect not only our mind but also our body. It can be difficult to sleep, eat or even concentrate on daily activities. But it's essential to find ways to overcome these difficulties and take care of yourself.

One of the most effective ways to take care of yourself is through self-care. This includes doing things that give you pleasure and allow you to relax, such as reading a book, watching a movie or series, taking a hot bath, going for a walk, or simply sitting and relaxing in a quiet environment. Self-care can also include meditation or yoga practices, which can help you connect with yourself and find inner peace.

Additionally, it's important to maintain a healthy sleep and eating routine. During grief, it can be difficult to sleep or eat, but it's crucial to do your best to maintain these routines. Proper sleep and a healthy diet help maintain physical and mental health, as well as provide energy to deal with emotional pain.

Another way to take care of yourself during grief is to seek emotional support. This may include talking to friends and family about your feelings, participating in support groups, or seeking professional help, such as therapy or counseling. There's no shame in asking for help, emotional support can help you deal with the pain of grief.

Finally, it's essential to give yourself time and allow yourself to go through the grieving process. Each person has their own time and way of dealing with loss. Don't pressure yourself to "get over it" quickly, but allow yourself to feel and experience the pain, knowing that, over time, you'll find peace and healing.

Remember that you're not alone, and there are many people and resources available to help you take care of yourself and find inner peace.

# CHAPTER 11

# SADNESS
# THAT COMES AND GOES

SADNESS IS AKIN TO THE SEA'S WAVES, EBBING AND FLOWING, YET YOU REMAIN STEADFAST ON THE SHORE OF YOUR OWN STRENGTH.

Sadness is one of the most intense emotions that we can feel. When we are going through a grieving process, it is very common for sadness to manifest itself intensely and constantly, appearing and reappearing. It is important to understand that feeling sad is normal and part of the healing process.

In the grieving process, it is common for sadness to be accompanied by a feeling of emptiness. The sensation that something is missing is constant and seems never-ending. In addition, it is common to feel a sense of hopelessness and difficulty in concentrating on other activities.

Sadness can also manifest physically, such as body aches, constant fatigue, loss of appetite, and insomnia. These symptoms are very common in people who are going through a grieving process and can last for a prolonged period.

It should be understood that sadness is part of the grieving process and it is necessary to live it intensely so that we can overcome it. Denying sadness can prolong the grieving process and prevent emotional healing.

On the other hand, it is important not to sink into sadness and seek help when necessary. Talking to friends, family, or even a health professional can help deal with sadness and find new ways to cope with loss.

Over time, this sadness can be transformed into a fond memory of the person we lost. It takes patience and care with oneself to be able to overcome the pain of grieving.

# CHAPTER 12
# ETERNAL LONGING

LONGING
IS EVIDENCE
THAT LOVE NEVER
TRULY PERISHES;
IT LIVES
WITHIN EVERY
REMINISCENCE.

When we lose someone important in our lives, long-ing can become even more intense and painful. The death of a loved one is one of the most difficult experi-ences we can face, and longing is one of the inevitable consequences of this process. When someone we love dies, we feel the absence of that person's physical pres-ence in our lives. Not being able to talk, hug, hear their voice, or feel their touch can be extremely painful.

Longing can make us question the meaning of life and leave us lost in our thoughts. It is important to re-member, however, that longing is also a proof of love and that that person left an indelible mark on our lives. It is natural to miss someone who was a part of our story and who left such significant memories. It is a sign that the person left a legacy that remains alive in our hearts.

Often, longing can make us think about how good it would be if that person were still here. We may find our-selves wishing to relive moments from the past or do things we didn't do while the person was still with us. It is important to remember that we cannot change the past and that death is an inevitable part of life. Instead of focusing on the absence of that person, we need to find ways to honor their memory and keep alive the leg-acy they left in our lives.

Some people find comfort in keeping objects that belonged to the person who passed away, such as clothes, photos, or letters. Others prefer to keep the person's memory alive by sharing stories and memories with friends and family. Some people also find solace in activities that the person enjoyed doing or in getting involved in volunteer work related to the cause that the person supported.

It's important to remember that each person deals with longing in a different way and that there is no right or wrong way to do it. It is a unique and personal process that can take time and requires care and understanding. It is important to allow yourself to feel the longing and not try to suppress or deny this feeling. It is normal to feel sad, lonely, and even angry at times. But it is also important to allow yourself to find comfort and support in the people around us.

Finding ways to deal with the longing and honor the memory of the person who has passed away can help in the acceptance process and in building a new meaning for life after loss. This can be done in various ways, such as visiting places that were important to the person, doing activities that he or she enjoyed, or even keeping objects that remind you of the person close by. The important thing is not to try to escape from longing, but to learn to live with it and transform it into something positive.

Facing and living with longing can be one of the hardest parts of the grieving process, but it can also be an opportunity to grow, learn, and build new meanings for life. It is impossible to erase the pain of loss, but it is possible to transform it into something positive and constructive to move forward with more strength and resilience.

Longing will be a constant reminder of the loved one who has passed away, but it can also be an impulse to keep living, loving, and honoring the lives of those who have already gone.

# CHAPTER 13

# THE SEARCH FOR A NEW MEANING IN LIFE

IN THE PURSUIT
OF NEW MEANING,
WE UNEARTH
THAT LIFE
CONTINUES
TO UNVEIL BEAUTY
AND PURPOSE.

When we lose someone we love, it is natural to feel confused and unsure how to move forward. The pain of loss can be overwhelming and often leads us to question the meaning of life and our place in the world. It is at this moment that many of us begin to search for a new meaning, for a reason that justifies the pain we are feeling.

This search for a new meaning is a very personal and unique process that can take time and require a lot of reflection and self-knowledge. Many people find comfort in religion or spiritual beliefs, while others seek a greater purpose for their lives through volunteering, involvement in social causes, or creating projects that can help others going through similar situations.

However, it is important to remember that the search for a new meaning is not an easy task and may not always bring clear and definitive answers. It is possible that during the grieving process, many questions arise and leave us even more confused and anxious. But it is important to persevere in this search, even if it seems like we are walking in circles, because it is through it that we can find a new purpose for our life and a new meaning for the loss we have suffered.

Some people also find comfort in sharing their stories with others who have gone through similar situations. The exchange of experiences can be very enriching and help in the understanding of our own grieving process and in the discovery of new paths and possibilities.

Finally, it is important to remember that the search for a new meaning in life is not a task that should be done alone. It is essential to have the support of friends, family, and qualified professionals such as psychologists and therapists who can help in the process of reflection and self-knowledge and in the understanding of the emotions and feelings that arise during grief.

Together, we can find a new path and a new meaning for our life after the loss of someone we love.

# CHAPTER14
# **SPIRITUALITY**

IN SPIRITUALITY,
WE FIND A HAVEN
OF PEACE AND
HOPE,
REMINDING US THAT
WE ARE PART
OF SOMETHING
GRANDER.

Spirituality is a vast concept that transcends the confines of traditional religions. It encompasses the quest for meaning, connection, and purpose in life. This pursuit can take on various forms, ranging from engagement in structured religious practices to individual exploration of spirituality through meditation, contemplation, or even moments of stillness and introspection.

When we confront the loss of a dear one, spirituality can serve as a compass guiding us through the labyrinth of emotions that accompany grief. It offers a pathway to discover a sense of significance amidst overwhelming sorrow. Spirituality beckons us to ponder profound questions about life, death, and what might lie beyond this earthly realm.

Death, an undeniably universal experience, often prompts us to ponder our very existence. It reminds us of life's transience and can lead us to contemplate what unfolds after we depart this world. Spirituality becomes a lens through which we can explore these inquiries, extending solace through beliefs in the continuation of the soul or in a spiritual existence after death.

For some, spirituality is a sanctuary where they find answers to these existential queries. This can impart a sense of inner peace and serenity, affording a broader perspective on the cycle of life and death. Moreover, spirituality can thread individuals into a fabric of shared beliefs, fostering a sense of community and support during moments of loss.

However, it is crucial to comprehend that spirituality isn't a universal panacea. The process of grieving is profoundly personal and intricate. Some may find solace in spirituality, while others may feel uneasy or not find meaning through it. Each individual has their own path to traverse and distinct ways of confronting the ache of loss.

Spirituality is not a shortcut to surmounting grief. While it may offer a framework to comprehend and confront loss, it doesn't exclude the challenging emotions that accompany the journey. Sadness, anger, and emptiness persist even within the spiritual sphere. Yet, spirituality equips us with tools to navigate these emotions and discover a sense of inner tranquility, even when the darkness of grief feels overwhelming.

Irrespective of how spirituality is practiced, whether through religious rituals, meditation, or any other form of spiritual connection, it can be a wellspring of support and solace. It provides a means to honor and remember those we've lost, while reminding us that the voyage of grief is uniquely personal for each individual.

# CHAPTER 15
# THE FEELING OF GUILT

LIBERATE YOURSELF FROM THE BURDEN OF GUILT; THE JOURNEY OF HEALING COMMENCES WHEN SELF-FORGIVENESS IS EMBRACED.

When dealing with the loss of someone important in our lives, it is common to feel a series of intense emotions. One of them is guilt, which can manifest itself in various ways and be a major obstacle in the grieving process. Let's explore this complex emotion and understand how we can deal with it in a healthy way.

Guilt is a common emotion in grief and can arise for various reasons. Often, we feel that we could have done something to prevent the death of the loved one. It may be that we had an argument with them shortly before their departure, and we feel guilty for not being more kind or loving. Or perhaps we blame ourselves for not spending more time with them while they were still alive, or for not doing enough to help them in difficult times.

Regardless of the cause, guilt can be a very painful and exhausting emotion. It can lead us to question our choices and feel incapable of moving forward. Therefore, it is important that we learn to deal with it in a healthy way.

One of the most important things we can do when dealing with guilt is to recognize that it is part of the grieving process and that we are not alone in feeling it. Many people who have lost someone important in their lives experience guilt in one way or another, and knowing this can help us feel less isolated.

In addition, it is important to understand that guilt is not always rational or justified. It is common for us to blame ourselves for things that were not under our control, or for not doing something that simply was not possible at the time. In these cases, it is important to try to change our perspective and see the situation in a more realistic way.

Another thing we can do to deal with guilt is to talk to someone we trust. This can be a friend, a family member, or a mental health professional. Talking about our feelings and concerns can help reduce the intensity of guilt and give us a clearer perspective on the situation.

It is also important to practice self-compassion and remember that we are fallible human beings, subject to making mistakes and facing challenges. Instead of judging ourselves harshly, we can treat ourselves with kindness and compassion, acknowledging that we are doing our best.

Finally, it is important that we learn to forgive ourselves and others. Forgiveness does not mean forgetting what happened or minimizing the pain we feel, but rather recognizing that we are all human and that, no matter how difficult it may be, we can find a way to move forward and find meaning in our lives again.

Dealing with guilt is not easy, but it is important that we learn to do so in order to move on with our lives and honor the memory of those we have lost. Guilt can be an obstacle, but with time, patience, and love, we can overcome it and find a new sense of purpose in our lives.

# CHAPTER 16
# THE ROLE OF THERAPY

IN THERAPY,
WE DISCOVER
THAT WE NEED
NOT FACE GRIEF
ALONE; HANDS
ARE EXTENDED
TO AID US.

Therapy is a powerful tool to help people in difficult times, such as in the case of grief. The role of the therapist is to assist the patient in exploring their emotions, finding healthy ways to cope with loss, and developing skills to manage stress and anxiety.

One of the greatest benefits of therapy is the safe space it provides for emotional expression. Many people have difficulty sharing their emotions with friends and family, for fear of being judged or burdening others. The therapist is a trained professional to deal with emotions and provide a welcoming and non-judgmental environment.

There are different therapeutic approaches that can be effective in treating grief. Cognitive-behavioral therapy (CBT), for example, is an approach that helps the patient identify and change negative thoughts and behaviors that may be contributing to their pain and suffering. Grief therapy focused on meaning reconstruction (GTMR) is another approach that focuses on helping the patient find a new meaning for their loss and build a new narrative for their life.

Regardless of the chosen therapeutic approach, the role of the therapist is essential to help the patient deal with their loss. The therapist can help the patient:

Understanding and accepting your emotions: Often, people try to deny or suppress their emotions related to grief, which can lead to emotional problems later on. The therapist can help the patient understand and accept their emotions without judgment.

Developing skills to cope with stress and anxiety: Grief can be a period of great stress and anxiety. The therapist can teach skills to deal with these emotions, such as relaxation techniques, meditation, and mindfulness.

Identifying negative thought patterns: Grief can lead to negative thoughts about oneself, others, and the world. The therapist can help the patient identify these negative thought patterns and find ways to change them.

Finding a new meaning for the loss: The therapist can help the patient find a new meaning for the loss and build a new narrative for their life. This can help the patient move forward with a more positive perspective.

Dealing with guilt and regret: Often, people who experience grief can feel guilt and regret about the person who passed away. The therapist can help the patient deal with these emotions and find ways to release these negative feelings.

Improving self-esteem: Grief can affect the patient's self-esteem. The therapist can help the patient develop a healthier self-esteem by recognizing their achievements and strengths.

In addition to these benefits, therapy can also help the bereaved person deal with practical and bureaucratic issues that may arise after the death of a loved one, such as dealing with wills, property issues, and finances. The therapist can help the bereaved person navigate these issues effectively and provide emotional support during the process.

Grief therapy can help the bereaved person find a new sense of purpose and meaning in their life after the loss of a loved one. The therapist can help the bereaved person explore their values, goals, and objectives and find ways to honor the memory of their loved one while moving forward in their own life. Therapy can help the bereaved person build a new identity, adapt to changes in life, and find meaning and purpose after loss.

# CHAPTER 17

# **OVERCOMING**

OVERCOMING
IS NOT
THE CESSATION
OF PAIN, BUT THE
COMMENCEMENT
OF CRAFTING
A NEW LIFE.

Life can be an emotional rollercoaster, with ups and downs, moments of joy and sadness. At some point, we all go through difficulties and challenges that seem insurmountable. When faced with adverse situations, it is normal to feel lost, desperate, and hopeless. However, overcoming is possible and can be one of the most enriching experiences of life.

Overcoming is the ability to face and overcome the adversities of life. It is the process of recovering emotionally, mentally, and physically after a challenging situation. Although overcoming may seem difficult, it is possible and can be achieved with the right tools.

To overcome a challenge, it is important to accept and understand the situation you are in. In many cases, denial can be a barrier to overcoming. It is common to deny reality and try to ignore the problem, but the truth is that denial can prolong the pain and delay the healing process. Instead, it is important to recognize the situation and allow yourself to feel all the emotions it brings.

Allowing yourself to feel is one of the most important things we can do when facing adversity. Pain, sadness, anger, and fear are natural emotions and are part of the healing process. It is important to allow yourself to feel these emotions and express them in a healthy way, whether through writing, art, music, or therapy. There is no magic formula for dealing with emotions, but it is essential to keep in mind that it is normal to feel sad, angry, or afraid, and that these emotions are part of the process of overcoming.

Another important point in overcoming adversity is seeking the support of family, friends, and mental health professionals. There is no shame in asking for help, and it is essential to understand that no one can overcome a challenge alone. Emotional support can help alleviate pain and loneliness and provide a network of emotional support.

In addition, seeking pleasurable activities can also aid in the process of overcoming. Doing something we enjoy can bring a sense of normality and help distract the mind from the pain. This may include hobbies, physical exercise, volunteering, or other activities that bring pleasure and satisfaction.

Overcoming is not a linear process and can have ups and downs. It is important to remember that recovery is not a race, but a personal journey. Sometimes it may seem like we are taking one step forward and two steps back, but that is normal and part of the process. Overcoming is a skill that can be learned and practiced and can bring a sense of achievement and empowerment.

Finally, it is important to remember that overcoming challenges does not mean that the pain will disappear completely. The goal is not to forget the adversity, but rather to find new meaning in it and build a new life narrative from it. Overcoming challenges is a continuous process that involves ups and downs, progress and setbacks. It is important to be patient and compassionate with oneself, allowing oneself to feel the emotions that arise along the way.

# CHAPTER 18
# THE LEGACY

THE LEGACY
OF THOSE
WE CHERISH
THRIVES IN
OUR ACTIONS,
INSPIRING US
TO LIVE
WITH PROFOUND
SIGNIFICANCE.

The legacy of grief is something that is often forgotten or overlooked during the process of mourning and suffering. However, it is important to remember that grief can leave a positive and meaningful legacy in our lives.

First and foremost, grief teaches us about our own resilience and inner strength. When we go through difficult times, we often surprise ourselves with our ability to cope with pain and overcome difficulties. Grief can be a testament to this, showing us that we are capable of dealing with something that once seemed impossible.

Moreover, grief can teach us about the importance of our relationships and connections with other people. When we lose someone we love, we often realize how much that person meant to us and how much our life was impacted by them. This can lead us to value our relationships even more and invest in them in a more conscious and loving way.

Another positive legacy of grief is the development of greater empathy and compassion for others. When we go through a loss, we know how difficult it can be and how overwhelming the pain can feel. This helps us to better understand the suffering of others and to be

more sensitive and compassionate to their pain and difficulties.

Additionally, grief can teach us about the importance of taking care of our mental and emotional
health. When we experience a loss, it is common to feel
lost, anxious, and depressed. This can lead us to seek
professional help and to learn new ways to take care of
ourselves and our emotional well-being.

Finally, the legacy of grief can be the creation of new
meanings and purposes in our lives. When we lose
someone we love, we often question the meaning of life
and our purpose. This reflection can lead to significant
discoveries and achievements, such as a career change,
seeking new relationships, or dedicating ourselves to a
cause that is important to us.

# CHAPTER 19

## HOPE

EVEN WITHIN
THE DARKEST
MOMENTS,
HOPE IS
THE LUMINARY
THAT STEERS
OUR PATH
OF HEALING
AND RENEWAL.

Life is a journey full of ups and downs, and at times, we may find ourselves lost and without hope. Situations such as the loss of a loved one, the end of a relationship, or professional failure can leave us shaken and disheartened. However, it's important to remember that there's always a light at the end of the tunnel, and hope is what keeps us moving forward.

Hope is a powerful feeling that helps us maintain faith and believe that things will get better. It allows us to see beyond current difficulties and have confidence that better days will come. It's a feeling that keeps us motivated and helps us keep fighting, even when things seem impossible.

But how can we cultivate hope in our lives? Is it possible to learn to have hope even in difficult situations? The answer is yes. There are strategies and practices that can help us nurture this feeling within us.

The first one is to learn to deal with negative emotions. When we find ourselves in a difficult situation, it's natural to feel emotions such as sadness, anger, and frustration. However, if we don't know how to deal with these emotions, they can turn into feelings of hopelessness and helplessness. It's important to allow ourselves to feel these emotions, but it's also important to learn to deal with them in a healthy way. Therapy can be a great option for learning to deal with negative emotions and finding positive ways to express them.

Another strategy for cultivating hope is to learn to be grateful. Even in the midst of a difficult situation, there's always something to be grateful for. It can be something simple, like having a roof over our heads or having friends and family who love us. When we learn to appreciate these things, our perspective changes, and we begin to see things in a more positive light. Gratitude is a powerful tool for cultivating hope in our lives.

When we're going through a difficult situation, it can be hard to see a better future. However, it's important to set realistic goals that allow us to see a way forward. These goals don't have to be big or complex, they can be simple things like starting a new hobby or enrolling in a course of studies. When we have realistic goals, we have something to strive for, and that helps us maintain hope.

Finally, it's important to seek support from friends and family. Loneliness can make us feel desperate and hopeless. When we connect with other people, we find emotional support, and that helps us maintain hope i difficult times. Additionally, being surrounded by positive and loving people helps us maintain a positive perspective and believe that better days will come.

# CONCLUSION

Grief is one of the most painful experiences we can face in life. It is a journey that we all go through at some point, but each person experiences it uniquely. It is important to remember that there is no right or wrong way to deal with grief, and that each person has the right to process it in a way that is healthy and meaningful for them.

In this book, we explored what grief is, the different phases of the grief process, and some ways to deal with grief in a healthy way. I hope that this book has provided some guidance and comfort for those who are going through grief or helping someone who is going through it.

Remember that it is important to allow yourself to feel your emotions and seek support from others, whether it's in a support group, with friends and family, or with a mental health professional.

Taking care of yourself and finding healthy ways to deal with grief can help you find meaning and purpose in life after the loss of a loved one.

You are not alone, and there is always hope for healing and recovery. Grief can be a difficult journey, but it can also offer the opportunity to grow and find deeper meaning in our lives.

With kindness and gratitude,

Leonardo Tavares

# ABOUT THE AUTHOR

Leonardo Tavares, at the age of 39, emerges as the esteemed author of the poignant masterpiece "Surviving Grief." A devoted father to a captivating 7-year-old daughter, he found himself widowed tragically at 36 years, when his beloved wife succumbed to a rare mediastinal cancer. Her tender age of 27 had only just been reached, marking a heart-wrenching loss.

The depths of sorrow are intimately known to Leonardo, who, through his personal journey, has acquired a profound understanding of the importance of allowing oneself to embrace all the emotions that arise during the process of mourning. He comprehends the arduous task of grappling with the longing and anguish that accompanies loss, and it is for this reason that he has chosen to extend a helping hand to others traversing this phase in their lives.

With his lucid and precise prose, Leonardo guides his readers towards the discovery of strength, courage, and hope during moments of profound sadness.

Assist others by sharing this remarkable work.

LEONARDO TAVARES

# Surviving Grief
## The Path to Your Resurrection

Milton Keynes UK
Ingram Content Group UK Ltd.
UKHW011102201123
432908UK00007B/1393